Two Ducks
in Tuscany

Philippa Dunn & Virginia Painter

This is for Mum (Honi) and Dad (T) without whom we probably would never have discovered Siena at all. Grazi.

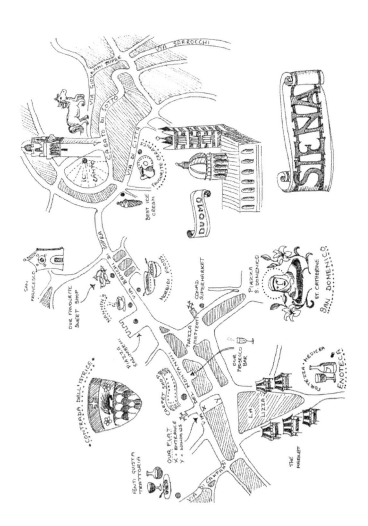

Prologue

I had to go back to Siena. I needed to go and say goodbye properly. I couldn't have known the last time I was there that it would be the last time, and so the end came abruptly and unexpectedly. The love affair had endured on memories and vague, unfulfilled plans to return, and now the time had come for it to blossom or die, depending. And all this without a man in sight. My love affair is with Tuscany in general and Siena in particular, because my parents had lived in the Tuscan countryside for many years and I had visited them regularly right from the start. Between the time they made the decision to leave and had actually packed up and moved out, I didn't get back to see them, and so I never really said goodbye to an important place and time in my life.

I knew exactly who would be the perfect person to do it with, too.

'Sprat? What about Siena?'

'What about it?'

'I really want to go back and wondered if you want to come.'

1

'Er.... yeah! Of course I want to come! When are we going?'

So we started to plan and decided that early June, before it got too hot, would be the perfect time for us both.

Sprat is my cousin; we've been best friends forever and because we've known each other and played together all our lives, we are the perfect travelling companions. Our first travelling adventure together was when we went to Venice (see Two Ducks in Venice) and now it was time for another adventure.

Since life is so short and the world so wide, the sooner you start exploring it the better

Simon Raven - The Spectator 1968

1.

I didn't give myself much time to get it all sorted so by the time I started hunting for a flat, I was coming across more and more of them with our desired week already booked. I was interested to find that you can rent a single room in a family home very easily, finding a whole flat for yourself is a little more difficult. Eventually I found the most amazing looking place, but it seemed unbelievably cheap, so I got into a correspondence with the owner and after a lot of misunderstanding and back and forth-ing, he agreed to rent us the whole flat with two of the 4 bedrooms locked, for a greatly discounted price. One thing we learnt in Venice is that renting a place with a balcony or a little private garden is a must, but this had neither. I couldn't afford to hesitate if I wanted it for our week, so against my better judgement I booked it, convincing myself it would be fine because the apartment was so huge and full of windows and wonderful views over the city. And besides, it was right across from the Lizza park so if we needed to get out and sit in the air, we'd be fine.

Our flight to Pisa left early in the morning, so we had to go to Gatwick the night before. I found a hotel that sounded nice, close enough to the airport but not beside the runway, and the price was great. I couldn't for the life of me find out how to book the bus from Pisa to Siena, so we decided it couldn't be that difficult and we'd figure it out when we arrived. Sorted.

I took the train to Gatwick south terminal and waited to meet Sprat who would fly in there too. As I watched the people pouring through the arrivals gate I couldn't help wondering about how little English I was hearing; plenty of German and Swedish and other languages I didn't recognise, but not a lot of English. At about the time when I was sure she should be through the gates someone behind me said,

'You're facing the wrong way.'

I'd been watching the European gate; the national flights came in behind me. Good start.

We got a cab to the hotel, and after we'd been driving for some time I broke off my conversation with Sprat and said to the driver

'Have I made a mistake booking this hotel?

Are we going to be too far away from the airport?'

'Oh no!' He smiled at me in his mirror. 'No mistake at all. It's a lovely hotel and you won't hear a single aeroplane all night. I bring many people here and it's very nice." And he was right. The Copthorne, it's called, and it seems to be set right out in the country. Beautiful gardens, dark wood counters with smiling staff, and two restaurants, and our room looked out over the lawns. Definitely no planes going overhead, either. The dinner we had was fantastic; we had the waiter and the chef to ourselves and the food was outstanding. If I thought I could ever find it again, I'd go there for a quiet getaway. Best of all, the shuttle bus to the airport runs all night, at 22 minutes past the hour; we needed to catch the 04.22 and it was right on time.

* * * * *

There aren't many airports left where you walk across the tarmac to the terminal from the plane, but Pisa is one of them. The air was hot – well, after England it was hot – and the heat came up from the tarmac and felt lovely. Chaos reigned in the luggage collection area and we watched people wander in and out of the hall, coming to meet people and stand about and chat. Eventually our bags came and we set off to find the bus, and the most extraordinary sequence of non-information encounters started. The lady in the ticket booth sold us our tickets to Siena, no problem, told us it left at 1p.m., and when we asked her where we got the bus she vaguely waved behind her and said something about 'outside' and 'right'. We had agreed that before we went anywhere we needed to eat something so we went to the largest and nearest source of food. We stood at the counter looking at the wonderful slices of pizza and smelling the coffee but no one came to serve us. The middle-aged ladies running the place were incredibly fast and efficient but seemed unable to see us. It was only when one of them took a moment off to have a little flirt with the delivery man that she noticed us, and then she indicated that we should have chosen what we wanted, gone to the till and paid, and then waited to be brought the food. She rather grudgingly scooped us out our pizza slices and then waved us over to the till where we managed to break the rules, ask for and get coffee, and then move off to one of the pillars with marble surrounds which serve as standing tables. A very good idea when you're in a hurry and/or encumbered with luggage. I'm not sure that the pizza was actually very good but it tasted delicious, and washed down with the most wonderful cappuccino, we both felt more able for the next bit.

We went outside and right, as instructed, glad to leave the chaos of Pisa airport, and found a little wall to sit on to sort ourselves out. We were surrounded by fragrant Mediterranean plants that gave us deep shade to sit in.

There were numerous buses of all shapes and sizes coming and going and after our little re-coup we headed for the most likely looking long-distance coach rather than a mini-bus. Sprat asked the driver if it was the bus for Siena. He looked at her blankly so she showed him our tickets.

'No, no! This is not the bus', he rattled off in Italian. 'Blah blah over there," he said, waving vaguely to the right and behind him. And so to the next bus, same question, same answer except that the arm wave was in a slightly different direction each time. I stood with the suitcases watching, strangely unperturbed. Our tickets said Siena so a bus would appear from somewhere, sometime.

By now Sprat had established that another couple who were wandering around looking confused in much the same way we were, were also trying to find a bus to Siena. They didn't speak any English but it was easy enough to figure out that we were both on the same mission. And then a bus came hurtling down the bus lane, threw itself round the corner and stopped on a dime about a foot from where we were standing. The door crashed open and a really wild looking bloke jumped out. His hair was dark, shoulder length, curly and all over the place; his eyes were blue and as wild as his hair, his shirt was untucked, shoes scuffed and his trousers had seen better days. The lit sign above the dirty windscreen said Siena. We had found our bus. It was a load-your-own-luggage set up, and try to find a seat that wasn't broken, and we ended up sitting in about the middle of the bus, the young couple behind us, and off the four of us went with our mad driver. Not long into our journey I nudged Sprat and pointed at the ceiling and we looked at each other, trying to contain our mirth. The ceiling had a wide strip of the same carpet that was on the floor of the bus. After a lot of discussion we decided this was so that in the event that the bus turned over, all passengers would feel they'd landed the right way up. In less extreme circumstances it probably just served to protect one's head when a particularly large bump was hit...

We learned two things on our race through the Tuscan countryside; *fazzoletti* is the word for tissues, and the best place to sit on the bus is up front, other side from the driver and then you can see the whole country in front and at both sides without cricking your neck. *Fazzoletti* we learned because the man of the couple approached us and asked us if we had any fazzoletti. I looked suitably puzzled and he took an empty tissue packet from his pocket and showed it to me.

'Ah! Tissues!' I said, leaping up and getting a little travel pack of tissues out of my bag and giving them to him. His pretty girlfriend thanked me profusely. Before I sat down, in my broken Italian I asked him what he had called them.

'Fazzoletti - Fa-zo-le-ti!' he said, index finger and thumb joined together, arm conducting each syllable, and once again he pulled the crumpled packed out of his pocket and showed me the word. I thanked him, we smiled and nodded and Sprat and I practiced the word for the rest of the way to Siena.

The drive to Siena was wonderful. The roadsides were thick and overgrown and full of wild flowers, most noticeable of course were the bright red poppies which seem to be able to grow just about anywhere. Umbrella pines lining the road for long stretches, villages with most of the window shutters down against the mid-day heat, and most Tuscan of all, the villages on top of the hills with tall, dark cypresses leading up to them. The fields were full of crops, there was evidence of some irrigation and with all this, hardly any people. It took us a while to realise that of course anyone with any sense at all was having a siesta.

Just before we started the climb up into Siena, our bus driver pulled over, and came down to talk to us. He asked us collectively where we wanted to get off, and our companions said 'statzione'. I know from somewhere that *stazione* means train station and not bus station, so I asked whether there was only one stop or could there be another.

To my huge relief he said "city centre" and after just a little hesitation I said yes, city centre. As he turned away I looked at Sprat.

'I'm sure that's what David said...' suddenly feeling very unsure.

'Have you got a text or email about it with you?'

'No... I have in my mind that we agreed that I would text when we arrived 'in the city', so I think that means the city centre. I know it's not the *stazione* because that's for trains.'

'Are you sure?'

'No...yes...I think so. Oh well, we'll text when we get to city centre and if it's wrong we'll just tell him where we are and hope he'll come and find us. Plan?'

'Plan.'

Note to self: *Really pay careful attention to the details of where your landlord is going to meet you!*

The bus drove up a winding, steep road that takes you inside the city wall, and immediately I began to feel as though I recognised it all, it felt so familiar. The bus station was obvious by the hoards of buses coming and going, and we climbed out and rather pointedly waited for our driver to get our cases out of the hold for us. They had been so thrown around on the drive that they had wedged themselves firmly against the far side of the hold, and I wasn't about to climb in and retrieve them. He got the message and very willingly did it for us. I texted David and then we wandered along the pavement in the deep shade of the lime trees, looking about and listening with delight to the Italian being spoken all around us. Just as I was about to text David again, a young man came towards us across the road, and said

'Dunn?'

'Yes! David?'

Tall, nice looking and smartly dressed in a pink shirt and chinos; we made the introductions and he led us off across the road, us talking in our broken Italian and he in his equally broken English. Just as we got across the road, David stopped and waved his hand upwards

'This the flat.'

We were standing outside an office supply shop and we both looked at him blankly.

'Right here?

'Yes! yes! Up!' he said, pointing up to the top of the building. And sure enough, there on the third floor the shutters and windows were wide open, inviting us up. Wow! When the ad said 'close to the bus station', it wasn't kidding. David led us down the side of the building, round the corner and there were the huge, solid doors we had seen on the web site. He unlocked and invited us into a lobby of marble and glass and wrought iron. The glass which made up the inside lobby door was etched with Deco roses. The floor and sweeping staircase were marble with beautiful wrought iron railings made to look like twisted rope with tassels at each end. On the floor,

 guarding the staircase, were two bronze griffins, with furled wings and the most amazing bosoms that looked just like modern implants. It was all old and slightly worn and a tiny bit musty but was magnificent and welcoming. Instead of heading up the stairs, David directed us to the left of the staircase down a narrow but well lit passage. We looked up and saw that the arched ceiling was painted in the most wonderful fresco of dancing ladies, flowers, shells and patterns of twiddles and twirls in rich red, blue and green.

'Wow! The colours are so strong! Has that been restored?' I asked.

David grinned.

'My...er... coo-san paint it!' I looked at him blankly but Sprat got it immediately.

'Your cousin! Wow, it's brilliant!'

'Yes, thank you.' He was delighted.

The lift he had been leading us to was tiny; we both squished in with our cases and David stood rather hesitantly at the door.

'Come in, come in, we can all fit!'

'All a bit cosy, but never mind...'

And off we went up to the third floor.

The door to the flat was right beside the lift on the left, the staircase down was straight ahead, and another apartment door on the right. Well, we think it was an apartment, but it had a wrought iron grille across the width of the lobby in front of it which seemed a bit alarming if it was a flat.

The flat and it was everything we'd hoped it would be. Tiled floors, domed, frescoed ceiling, heavy old hall furniture, and light pouring down the corridor from all sides. In the rather strangely furnished sitting room was a friend of David's, minding his own business and giving nothing away. David showed us around, we chose our rooms – both with a full ensuite – and we covered all the details of keys and money. Sprat started counting out her brand new, crisp euro notes and David made a comment about the new money.

'Yes,' said Sprat, 'we just printed it before we came.' David looked at us rather blankly, but his friend obviously understood because he had a huge grin on his face.

'We printed it – we made it', Sprat tried to explain, and then suddenly David got the joke and let out the most wonderful braying laugh which made us all laugh.

When eventually they left, we rambled round the

place, hardly able to believe our luck. We threw open the outside slatted plantation shutters and the windows in our rooms and the sitting room, flooding the flat with light and sound and sun. We went and inspected the kitchen and found all sorts of lovely things left by previous tenants and probably topped up by David. Our joy was complete when we both tried out our beds and found they were incredibly comfortable; what a relief that the nightmare of the Venetian sleeping arrangements would not be repeated - and how impossible it was to get up after the test, so we just stayed where we were and had a sensible little siesta.

* * * * *

When we finally emerged it was early evening. After a cup of tea – tea bags inherited – we wandered out with a view to finding the Campo before going to supper at a restaurant recommended by David. I had sort of got my

 bearings – medieval towns don't change much in 25 years – and we found the Campo with no trouble at all. From the street we went down a set of steep stairs with little shops on either side then

out we popped into Siena's central piazza. Oh, the joy of seeing it again, in all its magnificence. As huge as I remember, surrounded by medieval buildings, flats and houses with restaurants and cafes in their ground floor rooms. The Torre del Mangia presides over it all: the enormous clock at the base of the tower, white stone crenelated top and then on the very top of that, the huge, ancient bell that still rings. What a thrill to be back. There weren't many people in the campo that evening and we stood and just stared round it for a moment, transported back to another time. Knowing it would take quite a bite out of our kitty, we opted to have a welcoming drink at one of the bars on the Campo which we did, and we were right; a passable glass of wine at an eye watering price. Never mind – welcome back to Siena!

Sprat's sense of direction led us unerringly back to the flat which we then left behind us as we followed David's directions to find our restaurant. We passed wonderful little shops which must certainly rely on an established, local clientele. Vespas came and went past us and a few cars, but it may as well have been pedestrianised, there was so little traffic. And then we spotted our *Fonti Guista* trattoria and not a moment too soon. We were both hungry. We chose a table outside and were served by a charming young man who taught

us that when you ask for *vino di tavola per due* –
table wine for two – you will get two little half
litre carafes of, in this case, a lovely local wine.
Fresh bread and ferocious black olives before our
supper arrived, not a crumb of which was left on
the plates it was so delicious. We had to read and
re-read the bill because we couldn't believe that
such ambrosia could cost so little. €26.50 the bill
said. I suppose because our first dinner in Venice
had been so awful – €88 for a miserable fish and
dull polenta – we were half expecting the same
sort of disappointment, but it was not the case. It
was quite obvious right from the start that if the
food was this delicious and this inexpensive, we
wouldn't be doing nearly as much cooking as we
had in Venice.

Of course the walk home felt much shorter
than the walk to the trattoria. Sitting in the
kitchen of the flat with the windows wide open,
we could hear occasional squeaks from the swifts
that hadn't quite finished dining, and we looked
out over the roofs to the darkening sky.

'Apparently swifts never land and perch unless
they're feeding their young, did you know that?'

'I didn't,' said Sprat. 'Don't they sleep then?'

'They do; they fly really high and go into free
fall while they sleep, and they have a wonderful
built in alarm that wakes them before they get too
close to the ground. And while we're on a little
factoid safari, did you know that if a swift falls to

the ground it can't take off again, so unless someone picks it up and chucks it back into the air, it'll probably die of starvation.

'I did not know all that.'

'No, nor did I. Thank goodness for brainy brothers. Dad loved the swifts and he called them the Cossacks – I suppose because they wheel and shriek across the sky as they hunt, like the Cossack horsemen used to do. Anyway, whatever the reason, they've only ever been Cossacks to us.'

'Look!' said Sprat, pointing out of the window. Across the almost dark sky were two vapour trails that made a perfect cross.

'An angel's kiss for our first night; it's going to be a brilliant holiday.'

As I lay in my wonderfully comfortable bed after a perfect shower, and looked up at the old beams and terracotta tiles of my ceiling, I knew it would be a brilliant holiday, without doubt.

Once more on my adventure, brave and new.

Robert Browning, from 'Rabi Ben Ezra'

2.

When at last I woke, relaxed and completely refreshed, I padded down to Sprat's room, the marble tiles cool underfoot. She was awake and reading.

'Did you sleep well?'

'I did! You?'

'Brilliant thanks, not at all like Venice hey? Cuppa?'

'I've got one thanks. When I came past your room you were so fast asleep that I hated to wake you, and made myself a cup.'

In the kitchen I found evidence that Sprat had had one of the little crisp toasts with some butter and jam so I followed suit while the water boiled, and it was delicious. I drank my tea in bed while Sprat showered, and then we went out.

The morning was grey but dry, and we wandered along in the direction of the Campo, joining Banchi di Sopra, the main street, about half way down. We wondered whether, being Sunday, the shops would open later or at all, but we needn't have worried; the streets were full of people, some tourists in groups and some locals all gathering for a gossip and presumably either church or coffee. We found a little bar with tables on the side street and went in. Music was playing, an old gent was sitting at the back and the young lady was just getting organised for the morning rush. For very little money we got an enormous brioche and a hot, frothy cappuccino and sat up at the bar looking out of the open window on to the street. Unlike Venice, we weren't charged for sitting down. By the time we were ready to leave, the bar was filling up and the music had increased in volume – perfect timing.

We had been unable to find the little pop-up maps we had in Venice but our landlord had very thoughtfully left a map of Siena for us, and although it looked a bit like a paper place mat from a restaurant, it turned out to the be the most useful map until we could find something a bit more comprehensive.

On it we plotted our route to find where Mum and Dad had lived when they first arrived in Siena. They had taken a room in a house that catered for students because they themselves were students at the language school, – aged 60 and 54 respectively – with a view to becoming fluent in Italian before deciding where they would settle. I had forgotten the address, it was so long ago, but my brother remembered and we set off to find it. Leaving the Campo on our left we headed up the steep Via di Città trying to find street signs. More important than street signs are the little plaques indicating the *contrada* you're in. This is all to do with the famous Palio, and now I know a bit more about it, but for now suffice it to say that a *contrada* is the district of the town represented by a certain animal or symbol. There are 17 *contrade* and it is in the blood of all Sienese to take this very, very seriously. It would seem it's more important to know which *contrada* you are in

than what street you are on. Great for locals, slow going for visitors. Without being in a hurry we found what we were looking  for just as we were about to give up. Via Tito Sarrocchi, the address I had written to so often without being able to imagine it, and here we were. We walked up a little way and found what I'm sure was probably the same little grocery store Mum and Dad will have used as their local shop. We went in and made our way carefully past the tins and the bright shopping bags and the glasses and china to the vegetables and panforte all set out in their boxes. Hard pressed to choose, when we saw how crowded it was round the till with everyone having something to say on the current subject, we thought we'd leave our shopping and come back another time. We wandered back to the street and just like in Venice, getting lost is never something to worry about; if you can locate one landmark, like the Campo tower – Torre di Mangia - or the cathedral, you know more or less where you are and in no time will know exactly where you are.

Because Siena is built on hills, you keep getting little glimpses out over the town and into the countryside, which is not that far away, and in June still green and lush before the summer can take its toll.

We followed the road round and down the hill, under an arch in the old wall, and down a street with one or two cars parked on it and the same number of little shops open, and once the road had climbed back up, we could see the tower of the Campo. We knew where we were, and discovered we had almost walked a full circle and would end up in the Campo. Siena is a lot smaller than I remember.

The Campo is the main square in the town, and it is round this huge square that the Palio races twice a year. The floor of the Campo slopes downwards in nine paved 'segments' which were made to commemorate the Council of Nine, which governed Siena from the mid-13th century to the early 14th century. It was a time of stability and prosperity in spite of the council being judged by modern historians as 'self-seeking and profligate', and it was the period in which most of the city's public

monuments were built. On the high side of the square is the wonderful Fonte Gaia – fountain of joy – which is where St Catherine is reputed to have come to collect water for the hospital high up near the cathedral. All around the square the ground floors of the great buildings are mainly restaurants and some shops, taking up two thirds of the square. The bottom edge is the wonderful Palazzo Pubblico which is where the famous Torre del Mangia stands looking out over the whole town. A long queue and many hundreds of people later you can find yourself at the top of the tower looking out over Tuscany, but we opted to find another way to see the view and were glad we did. We meant to go into the Palazzo Pubblico which is the town hall and has been the home of the city authorities since 1310, but the queue and our hunger made us postpone the event, and we never did go back and do it. What we needed was some lunch, so forsaking the restaurants actually situated on the Campo because they were prohibitively expensive and too swept up for what we wanted, we wandered down a little side street on which were two rather less upmarket looking restaurants. We opted for the second of these and sat ourselves down outside. Eventually the very beautiful but sadly, as we were to discover, not very bright waitress came, and we ordered our drinks and a plate of mixed meats and olives to share. When that was finished we caught her attention again, and pointing to two items on the menu, ordered our next course. She seemed a little puzzled, so we pointed at the pictures by the name of the dishes and said 'questi' and thought that would be enough to get what we wanted. Ages later she returned with another plate of mixed meat and olives. Clearly my Italian is more rubbish than I thought, and the pictures are not sufficient guidance either, so we gave up trying to explain the mistake and waved her away saying 'bene, bene!' which even she could understand. The bill, of course, made us gasp but we had enough sustenance to get us home, and besides, the gentle rain had stopped and we would stay dry on the walk home to siesta.

Note to self *There really is never a good enough reason to eat or drink anything in the highest tourist catchment area except just to say you did.*

We walked across the Campo, up the steps and under the arch onto Via di Città. The shop on the corner caught our eye because it was called, for whatever reason, Pull Love. Contrary to what one might imagine, it sold mens' beautiful cashmere jumpers and silk scarves. We were idly window shopping when I stepped back slightly just as the man beside us stuck his right arm out, pointing to a poster in the shop window but looking at his friend on his left as he did so. His finger narrowly missed Sprat's eye and we both jumped back with exclamations.

'Oh! I'm so sorry!' he said in a thick Australian accent, and the conversation started. As soon as he and his friend and Sprat and I started talking, their wives wandered off and left them to it. We talked about how we each came to be in Siena, where they were staying, why we chose to stay in a flat – all the usual banter – and then the first guy, his wonderful handlebar moustache curling upward as he smiled, said

'By the way, my name is Bruce, and this is my friend Bruce.'

Running with the gag I said

'Hi Bruce – Bruce – my name's Sheila.'

Without missing a beat Bruce 2 said

'Oh, is that a real name?'

The burst of laughter that ensued didn't get a reaction from the Wives.

Bruce asked us if we knew the image in the poster. It was a picture of a young couple in a clinch on the ground with a line of police in hi-viz jackets in the background. According to Bruce it was taken during some riots in Canada and it was just a spontaneous moment of passion between two strangers. We debated how likely it was that it was spontaneous and not orchestrated to make a marvellous photo op, and soon Bruce and Bruce decided they had better move on, so we reminded them to buy 'Two Ducks in Venice', promised we'd write about them in 'Two Ducks in Tuscany', and said our goodbyes.

* * * * *

After a peaceful and rather long siesta, we decided it was time to go and buy some food. David had told us how to find the supermarket – Conad – and I vaguely remembered it from years ago. Heading in what we knew could only be the right direction we found ourselves in a piazza which I sort of recognised. The post office was on one side, but now there was a huge roundabout in the middle of the piazza and I would swear it wasn't there 25 years ago. I knew that if we walked across Piazza Matteotti Conad would be on the other side, but that had all changed a bit too, with some new building and reorganising. What I did recognise though was the little church on the corner, and right beside it was the entrance to the *galleria* – shopping centre. Conad was still downstairs, as it always had been, but now it was just a grocery store and not a great big general store as it had been.

It's so tempting to buy one of everything when you shop in the country that makes your very favourite food, so Sprat and I really had to try and contain our joy and buy only what we knew we would finish in the week. We bought some biscuits for dunking in our tea which were our only culinary mistake. They will forever be known to us a desiccated dog poo. No mind, we bought plenty of other delights.

I was going cook on the first night and had decided to make a one-pot-pasta which I had tried only once, with some success I thought. To the basket we added some chocolate, cheese, bread, fruit – peaches as hard as rocks – and two bottles of very cheap Chianti which turned out to be the only wine we bought the whole time we were there, it was so wonderful and about €20 later we set off home. We could tell even at this stage we were going to be torn between eating delicious food out for very little money, or buying and making our own delicious food for very little money. What a lovely surprise after Venice.

We felt that a glass of prosecco would be a nice way to start the evening, so we went to a bar further down our street and decided to sit outside in their very neat little piazza across from the bar.

We went in and ordered our prosecco which they said they would bring out to us. Sure enough, quite quickly our waiter appeared bearing two glasses and a bowl of crisps and we had been right; it did start our evening off perfectly.

We substituted ingredients I had used for ones we had to hand, and supper turned out surprisingly well. The recipe for the one pot pasta is at the back of the book - it's adaptable, and we both highly recommend it.

The clouds had cleared, the sun had set and the Cossacks were flying high to sleep when we went to bed, exhausted and completely happy.

Always wear corsets, to leave off wearing them at any time for the sake of coolness is a huge mistake: there is nothing so fatiguing as to lose one's ordinary support.

Constance Larymore from A Resident's Wife in
Nigeria, 1908

3.

The buses start running very early in Siena, as do the vespas which all park across the road from the flat along the edge of La Lizza, so there's no sleeping in. It's no hardship, though, to make a cup of tea, open the shutters to let in the light, shut the windows to keep out the sound and let the morning start without you. Today the plan was breakfast at Siena's most famous cafe, Nannini, on the Banchi di Sopra. We were early enough that the roaring trade they do with the local Sienese population had not yet started in earnest, and we had the pastry counter almost all to ourselves. We only had to contend with some beautiful American girls and their mother who were slow to decide and exhaustingly choosy. Sprat and I, on the other hand, know that there is no such thing as a horrid Italian pastry, so we just chose something we've never tried before – crisp orange pastries – ordered a cup of the wonderful Nannini coffee and moved away to sit at one of the four empty tables. Between us and the street was a huge glass window, and watching Siena come to life is a wonderful way to start the morning. Two elderly gents, immaculately dressed, their shoes shiny and their expensive but well worn hats tipped slightly back on their heads, wandered past, hands behind their backs, chatting idly to each other. A woman of indeterminate age, elegant and beautifully dressed, paced up and down in front of the window, completely oblivious to us as she checked her watch, looked up and down the street and checked her watch again. Not a good way for her to start her day, poor thing. By now the street was getting busy with people going to work, shops being opened, goods being delivered and hardly standing room at the coffee counter. We had timed it perfectly.

As we had done a little exploring the day before, we had a fair idea of where we wanted to start our shopping mission, namely pottery from Siena. But before we set off, I decided to text David and ask him which *contrada* we were in, because we thought it would be nice to buy at least one item with the appropriate animal on it. He texted back the word *istrice,* and as we had just walked into the first ceramic shop, I asked the owner for a translation.

'Istrice? that is porcupine, why you ask?'

'We're staying in the istrice contrada,' I explained, 'and we just wanted to know what it is.'

'Ah!' he beamed at us, 'the BEST contrada to be in! This is MY contrada also! Where are you staying?'

We told him and of course he knew exactly where we were talking about – he's probably a friend of David's actually, but was too excited about the *contrada* link 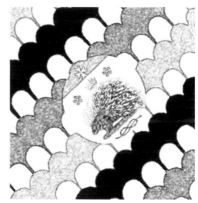 to say so – and the world of the Palio was opened to us there and then.

I've always known the importance of the Palio, but only now did I understand that it's not just a bareback horse race run round the Campo twice a year since the 13th century. It *is* Siena. It involves the entire city, all year long. Traditional Sienese only marry within their *contrada* and nothing, not war, famine or plague, can stop the Palio from being run. Even the council elections of 1919, when the Fascists were gaining ground, were postponed until after the Palio had been run. And it's not just about the people; if a riderless horse wins the race it gets a place of honour at the victory banquet and has its hooves painted gold. I remember being told by someone in Siena that all the riders are from Sicily because the Mafia promised to stay out of Siena as long as this was so. Whether this is true I don't know, but it is a good indication of the importance of the event and everything connected to it.

Only a few questions were needed to get our friend going, and we encouraged him by asking if *istrice* would win the Palio this year.

'Ha!' he said, 'we no need to win, we have won many times' – and he rattled off the years, going back to when he must have been a very small boy – 'but we must stop our enemy from winning, that is much more *importante*.'

'Your enemy?'

'Si! La lupa! – the she-wolf – she is the enemy of istrice for many years now.'

'Why, what happened?'

'In 1933 the istrice put a flagpole on a wall. La lupa said it was their wall, istrice of course did not agree and they fought for a long time about it. So, it went to court...'

'They went to court about a flagpole?'

'Si, to the Court of the Palio' (obviously) 'and the court ruled for istrice and la lupa has never forgiven us and we are enemies. We must stop la lupa from winning this year.'

The spark was in his eye and we didn't take this lightly.

Sprat asked 'Do all contrade have enemies?'

'Not all, but most. Some also have, er, how you say.... on the same side....'

'Allies?'

'Si, si! allies.'

'Who is your ally?'

'With us it is the goose.'

'I thought the she wolf was the symbol of Rome, but you see it everywhere here. Why is that?' I asked.

'Because-a, Siena was founded by Senius, he was the boy of Remus – you know them?'

'Romulus and Remus, yes.'

'Si. And also, the wolf in Rome, she look forward and the Sienese wolf, she look over her shoulder. Did you know this?'

'No, I didn't! I shall look more carefully.'

We asked whether you can only marry in your *contrada* and he said, no, people do marry outside now.

'So which contrada will the children belong to then?' we wondered.

'Well, one friend of mine, his father was from one contrada, his mother from another. They agreed that any girls would be from the mother's contrada, and any boys from the father's contrada.'

'That sounds fair doesn't it?'

'Ah si, it is fair, but for the poor mother, she have only boys!'

We talked on about how he was born in Siena

and had lived there all his life, and his brother also. He runs the ceramic shop – Ceramiche Artistiche Arcaico – in the morning, and then his brother, who runs their glass business – Vetrate Artistiche Toscane – in the morning, comes across

town and they swap places. Apparently they make all manner of wonderful glass for both private clients and for the city churches. 'The glass is in my blood,' he said. Then he laughed and held up his hand to show us a plaster on his palm and said 'Maybe my blood is in the glass also!'

We bought one or two little pieces and promised to return for more when we had shopped a bit, and we both looked forward to meeting him again. By the time we left, his brother had arrived to take over, and you would never have guessed they were related, they were so different.

As we shopped, we retraced our steps from the day before in order to find a shop on the Via Giovanni Dupre that Sprat had read about in a blog. Apparently it was wonderful and worth finding, but search as we might, we couldn't find it, so we carried on up to the Campo, crossed it and headed for the most amazing looking deli we had seen on our way out to Nannini's. Easy to find, Morbidi foods is something that I do remember from long ago, and as it's almost opposite Nannini's, it's easy to remember. The difficulty with a wonderful place like that is what to choose. Trays of cooked delicacies – artichoke hearts, rolled pork and herbs, little roasted shallots, roasted mixed meat – and then a counter of cold meats and pasta dishes and olives and tomatoes, and the same size again of cheese. The people who work behind the counter are delightful and hardly speak any English; it is definitely where the locals shop. Sprat finished paying – almost no money bought pecorino cheese, prosciutto, olives, ricotta, bread and fresh tortellini – and as we decided to stay and have a coffee before going home, David and his friend walked in.

When he'd got over his surprise at seeing us, David asked, 'How you know about the contrada?'

I explained about my parents living in Italy for many years and that I'd been to the Palio and I understood a bit about it all.

'Your parents lived in Siena?!'

'Well, they lived just near San Rocco a Pilli, just outside Siena.' He still looked a bit blank, so I said, 'Do you know San Rocco?'

He thought for a moment, and then said, 'Ah! San Rocco! that is in the country somewhere, si?' as he waved his hand over his shoulder as if brushing away a fly.

I laughed. Dad had often said that to a real Sienese, anywhere outside the wall was actually almost in another country, and I could see what he meant. David's friend, though, acknowledged that he knew San Rocco, and didn't seem surprised. Perhaps he'd been as far afield as Florence and was more worldly.

Sprat and I finished our delicious coffee and we took our food and presents home. The tiny lift in the apartment was being a bit temperamental and after being reluctant to start, it then lurched and bucked, making us rather round-eyed. We were happy to get out at the top and immediately forgot all about it, of course. We emptied all our shopping on to the sofa, and were pleased with what we'd bought. In Venice we had sworn that we wouldn't buy presents for everyone every time we went somewhere, and that the Venetian haul would be a one-off event. Of course when you find all these glorious things to buy, you immediately think of who would like it and the good intentions evaporate as the delights go into your bag. We took the groceries into the kitchen to make a delicious lunch of tortellini with lemon juice, oil, parsley and cheese – recipe in the back –

and found that the shirt Sprat had washed and hung on the line had blown off, down into the enclosed courtyard below.

'Oh no! Your shirt! It's in the courtyard downstairs!'

Sprat looked out of the window.

'Thank God it wasn't my big knickers!'

We decided we'd go and ask for it back on our way out after siesta.

When we went downstairs we rang the doorbell several times, but no one appeared.

We left the flat and walked across the road toward La Lizza park with a view to trying to find the place that Dad had brought all his grandchildren, years and years ago, on a drawing trip. He had decided they should all make an effort to learn to draw, so armed with pencils and pads and very little enthusiasm, we set off for the event. He had positioned them all around the wall looking down over the city and amid an awful lot of muttering and whispering, he had urged them on. He saw quickly that it was a futile effort and that a gelato was what everyone really wanted, so we packed up the drawing kit, chalked one up to experience, and went in search of a treat. I was certain I would recognise the dreaded drawing place the moment I saw it, but of course this much later the trees were bigger, grass had been planted etc. But I knew we were in the right place when I looked over the wall across the top of the town and out into the country. That much had hardly changed.

Leaving those memories behind us, we walked along the wall and unexpectedly came across an amphitheatre. Although it was empty, it looked far from abandoned and I imagine it may well still be used, perhaps for political rallies, maybe even concerts and plays. In hindsight I wish I had got Sprat to sit at the top and I had gone down to the bottom and we had experienced first hand how the acoustics really work. I could have put my great dramatic skills to the test...

Leaving it to our left we continued to walk round the wall on well kept gravel paths with tall shade trees on one side and wonderful rose beds on the other. Of course we stopped to smell the roses and both agreed that they smelt quite Italian and not like English roses at all.

We hardly saw a soul as we walked, but when we came back down to street level, we found ourselves in the middle of the huge upheaval of the fun fair leaving town. We had heard the noise of the fair for the past two nights but hadn't investigated, and now knew what it was. Huge lorries were being manoeuvred around medieval buildings, down narrow roads and round corners that a cart would have been cautious navigating. How these guys got themselves out, all in a long line and with no shouting or hooting – except with laughter – I don't know. While we were dodging between lorries, I noticed an entrance that seemed to go down into the base of the wall.

I was sure this was the Enoteca, a place I had been determined to find and show Sprat. The word enoteca translates from the Spanish as 'wine repository' Traditionally the primary focus of an Enoteca is to give visitors the chance to taste wines – mostly local – at reasonable prices with the opportunity to buy them by the bottle. I had been introduced to the Enoteca in Siena by Dad and I really wanted to share the experience with Sprat.

It occurred to me then that we must have been walking round the Fortezza Medicea, which of course we were. Built in 1560 by Cosimo 1 after his defeat of Siena, it forms part of the city wall, and it is indeed the home of the Enoteca and exactly where we wanted to be. It all came flooding back. We followed the path down to the entrance, but a delivery van blocked our way, and there didn't seem to be much activity inside either, so we made a plan to come back.

In our sights had been the Basilica di San Domenico, and now we headed purposefully in its direction. As we walked we looked at the countless posters of handsome politicians that had been stuck along the hoarding of a building site, one in particular – The Grey Suit – who we thought looked like a rogue, albeit rather a handsome one. Not being remotely interested in Sienese politics, we carried on to the magnificent basilica. There were so few people around the entrance that we weren't even sure if it was open to the public; in Venice the crowds advertise the venue. Not expecting to be allowed in we pushed the huge door open, and found ourselves in the dark cool interior of the most magnificent building.

Just as it had been in medieval times, there were no benches or seats of any kind. The tiled floor was shiny and worn, on the walls were enormous and beautiful paintings and frescoes, and huge and surprisingly modern stained glass windows. About half way down on each side of the room were candle holders with the requisite candles to be bought, lit and placed with a prayer or a thought. This we did; me for Dad and Mum, and Sprat for her friend. There were a few people in the church, many obviously local who came regularly, and a few tourists. Quite extraordinary to have a wondrous place like this almost to ourselves, especially after Venice. We wandered quietly through the cavernous hall and into the little gift shop where the tranquility of the church was broken by the loud voice of the assistant talking on the phone while he served a customer and continued a conversation with one of the priests. Sprat bought some little presents from among the glittery rosaries, crucifixes and the silver hearts and we went back into the church. I wanted to see the reliquary in which St Catherine's finger is supposed to be, but not only did I not find it, I've since been told it's not her finger but her head. I'm glad I didn't find it then.

Once outside, the steps led down the side of the building, and the view across the little valley of tree tops and roof tops to the  Duomo is quite breathtaking. I looked carefully at the steps because I was looking for a little black marble cross that I remember seeing last time I was in Siena, and I remember that it was meant to commemorate the place St Catherine had fallen and broken a tooth. I knew these weren't the right steps, but I couldn't remember where the right ones were. Questions would have to be asked.

Slowly we started for home. Before turning off Via dei Montanini and crossing the piazza to Conad, we saw that the most wonderful carpet shop, Mascagni, was open. This happened to us the whole week; we could walk down a street every day and the same shops were seldom open twice. This is wonderful in a way because it means there's a surprise every day, but on the other hand it's very annoying if you plan to go back next day and all you can find are shutters that blend in perfectly with the wall so you start questioning whether you're even in the right place. This shop was huge by any standards but especially for Siena, and after we'd both admired one of the Persian carpets in the window, we decided we should go in and see what was what. The prices seemed incredibly low – €245 for a big, beautiful Persian carpet – and as we both love carpets as the best way to decorate a house, we thought we might find something we couldn't resist. The gentleman who came out to greet us was immaculately dressed and very polite and had enough English to understand our interest in the one carpet in particular. He told us a bit about it and then turning to Sprat, asked where she was from.

'England', she said.

'From which part?'

When she said she was from Cornwall he couldn't have cared if I was from Mars, he was so delighted. Apparently he had been to England with his wife and brother and sister-in-law and they had traveled mostly in Cornwall and was completely enamoured with it. We had to slowly ease ourselves round the room in order to see what else he had in his cave of wonders, and the rooms just went on, one after another in an extraordinary and quite unexpected way. We could have spent a day and a fortune in there with him, but after he raced away and came back with a rather battered map of England to show Sprat where he had traveled, we thought we might consider it all a bit more. He gave us his card and urged us – Sprat – to return any time. If I'd thought for a moment I could have found the perfect spot for the carpet, I would have had it – something I never expected in Siena.

At Conad we bought supper ingredients and a few extras, and when we dropped them at home we went to see if anyone was in downstairs so we could try again to retrieve Sprat's shirt. No luck. We went back to our little piazza for our evening prosecco and this time it was served with  strawberries, chips and peanuts '...because you are

Eengleesh.' Well, obviously that would be our evening stop from now on.

Supper – Sprat's turn to cook – was tortellini with lemon and parsley and was just perfect – recipe in the back – and we spent the evening in the kitchen with the window wide open and watched the sun set as the Cossacks called it a day and stopped their wheeling and shrieking. Plans for tomorrow would wait until we had a coffee and pastry settled in front of us.

The true wanderer, whose travels are happiness, goes out not to shun, but to seek.

Freya Stark (1893-1993)

4.

A gentle stroll down to Nanini's seemed like the obvious answer to the breakfast question, and just as we turned from the counter to find a table, a group of people surged through the door, all talking at once. A rather short, beautifully dressed, silver haired gent was the centre of all the excitement and when Sprat and I recognized him, we couldn't help smiling at each other. Our handsome, debonair bill-board politician was standing right there in front of us, enjoying every moment of the attention. But his skin was sallow, he was shorter than Sprat and he had a very unfortunate habit of licking his lips as though he was very nervous. Oh, how disappointing! And what a great job the makeup artist had done for his photoshoot. I'm sure this is not the first time the observation has been made that some politicians are not what they seem.

After our heavenly custard cream and wonderful coffee we went back to the Via di Città to find Grafiche Tassotti, the shop that sells the most beautifully made paper product: notepaper and envelopes and notebooks and box files to name a few. Mostly the designs are classic Florentine patterns of bright colours and gilding, and they are quite intoxicating. I bought a packet of very useful notelets and matching envelopes to give as a little gift to someone, but am glad I have since persuaded myself to keep them.

From there to our pottery shop where the older brother was in charge for the morning. We talked about Siena and the things we'd seen and then I asked him

'Somewhere in Siena there is a marble step with a little black marble cross inlaid into it, which is meant to be where St. Catherine slipped and chipped her tooth. Can you tell us where it is?'

'Ah!' he laughed gently and waved away my question. 'The Sienese, they like to make up stories, you know? That is not where she chipped her tooth. No! that is where she levitate!'

Once we'd all stopped laughing at this wonderful story, he told us the step did indeed exist and where to find it. Not far from his shop, in fact, the step was one of the long steep set of stairs leading up to the Duomo (cathedral). Sure enough we found the beautiful little black marble cross inlaid in the white marble step, and we both sat down, one on either side of it, just to be there for a moment, and see if we might levitate too. We took the requisite pictures (I was closer to levitation than Sprat, it must be said) and then we noticed that there were all sorts of people sitting down on the steps and enjoying the view down into the town and over the roofs into the country. We had started a trend.

From there we went into a gallery which was actually under the cathedral in the crypt, and what an amazing place it was. Frescoes – probably dating from about 1280 – fading on the walls and not being restored; huge marble statues of obviously important men, with extraordinary posture and surprisingly roughly carved features. We wondered about these things as we walked around the almost empty gallery – what a blissful change from Venice – and finally decided that the bent heads and rounded shoulders are because originally these statues would have been around the top of a huge room – maybe the Cathedral itself – looking down on the people below, and perhaps their features were so coarse because if they'd been any finer they would be indistinguishable from the ground. Of course the way to find out about these things is to buy the guide books available in the town and around the cathedral, but we just took ourselves round and although we missed some key pieces, we saw some wonderful pieces too, and it does give you a different sense of it all, more like an atmosphere and an emotion than a structured tour and an art history lesson.

We carried on up the hill, through the arches that defined the boundaries of the cathedral at one time, and we joined the queue to climb high up inside the wall and get a view over the city and the surrounding countryside. Originally the cathedral was designed to be the largest church in the country, to be built in the design of a Latin cross. The north–south transept was completed and work started on the east–west nave but the plague

halted the work, which was never resumed. The wall we were about to climb to the top of was the beginning of the incomplete east wall of the Duomo. This was to be our answer to the Torre di Mangia in the campo, which we had decided against because of the queues and crowds. A good decision. When we got inside and up the first level, we found there were very few people queuing in front of us waiting to go up. We did wonder whether this was because our timing was perfect and we'd beaten the crowds, or because it wasn't worth the effort and we were among the few who didn't yet know that. We chatted to the couple in front of us while we waited, and as they were sure we would be riveted by their tales of travel and Property Bond accommodation, they made sure they didn't leave out a single story.

Eventually our guide gave us a little talk about what we could expect.

'There are 146 steps,' she said, and smiled mischievously. What she failed to say was that the 146 steps were the first part of the climb, after which there were several more to the higher point! But for all that, it was worth it. We climbed the 146 steps and gasped, not only from breathlessness, but at the wonder of the view in front and below us. We were in a very narrow sort of tunnel without a roof, which was a part of the wall round the cathedral. The guide urged us on, into a little dark doorway and up another tiny curving stairway, and then we arrived where we were meant to be: on the very top of the wall round the Duomo with the most spectacular 360 degree view around us. The tiled roofs below us were so close together they seemed almost to touch each other and the streets weren't visible, except right below us. The break between the end of the roofs and the beginning of the countryside was abrupt, and I saw clearly for the first time just how small Siena really is. Interestingly, right in front of us an enormous cedar tree rose out of the buildings and towered over the rooftops; the only other green to be seen in the city were a few

potted plants on balconies. The other interesting feature was the number of skylights of all shapes and sizes that had been let into the ancient roofs. Big and small, single and clustered, they must have brought some welcome light into the otherwise close and darkened buildings. We were able to walk to the end of the parapet and get the full view of the city and a stretch deep into the Tuscan hills, and then we turned and we were almost eye level with the top of the cathedral, its roof slightly below us, the third floor of its magnificent black and white bell-tower at our eye level. The cars and people below us were tiny and unaware, and if some of our companions had been better behaved it would have been a peaceful and secret view of the world around us.

Note to self: *Siena is not the ideal destination for small children; if travelling with grandchildren, stay in the country and visit the town for a day at a time, just as we did when our children were small.*

On our way down the stairs I stopped and took off my flip-flops and went barefoot; the steps are so narrow and so tight that I really got a bit nervous about losing my footing. When we got back to the line of people waiting to go up, it snaked right back along the passage, round the corner and to the top of the entry stairs.

This little adventure deserved a reward of a gelato so we made our way back down to Via di Città and into the little gelataria we had been eyeing on our shopping forays. If you're going to indulge, go all the way. We chose chocolate lined, nut encrusted, double scoop delights. Mango, peach and hazelnut for me, coconut and lemon for Sprat, and not a calorie between us. Heaven. As we stood on the corner of the street watching the world go by, a middle-aged man with an unfortunate habit of licking his lips held up the flow of pedestrians by insisting on taking several photographs of a passerby's little dog. Much later in the day, in a completely different part of the town, we saw him again, still licking his lips, which just goes to show how small Siena is.

The little lift lurched and rattled us back up to the flat and imagine our squeals of delight when we stepped out to find Sprat's shirt hanging on the door handle! I suppose it was inevitable that the people downstairs would go out into their courtyard and find the shirt eventually, but still it was a lovely surprise to see it back. After a celebratory glass of Chianti and a lunch of potato and rosemary pizza, prosciutto, pecorino, tomatoes and chocolate, we needed a siesta and of course there's no point fighting these things.

When we got into the lift that evening, Sprat said 'Brace yourself!' before she pressed the button. 'Brace yourself' turned into 'Bruce yourself' and our trusty little lift was Bruce thereafter.

Our evening stroll took us away from our usual bar and through the park to the Enoteca.

When I had been here before, many years ago, it consisted of a long nondescript hall filled with tin tables and chairs, and a bar. You could choose a wine from anywhere in the country and try a glass of it for almost no money. No food was served and you could bring your own sandwiches and snacks to help soak up your experiments. We had some sandwiches. I suspect this is why it's all changed now; you can drink a huge amount in a very short time – there are a lot of vineyards between Venice and Sicily –

and quite soon find yourself weaving back to your car, laughing at nothing at all, and endangering everyone by driving home. In the late seventies there were hardly any cars on the road which is probably why I'm still here to tell the tale. But now the Enoteca is new and much more sophisticated. The decor is understated and elegant, the staff in starched white shirts and black suits, and there are only half a dozen wines from Tuscany to sample by the glass, otherwise you buy a bottle.

We were taken to sit outside in the most beautiful sanctuary-like garden with high, ancient walls on three sides, the sun just kissing the top of one of them, the cloudless blue sky beyond. We were two of only four people there so it was quiet and peaceful, the only music coming from the blackbird in an overhanging branch. Enormous terracotta pots planted with climbing roses, olive trees and geraniums filled the little courtyard with colour and scent, and the iron tables and chairs, the crumbling brick in the walls and the ancient uneven herringbone brick floor almost completed the perfection. The ambrosial prosecco for only €4 a glass topped it all off. We took out our pads and pencils all ready to do some sketching but we abandoned it half way through our first glass of prosecco, giving over to the peace and loveliness of the evening instead.

Because the ethos of the Enoteca is to market Italian, and particularly Tuscan, wines, we asked about the prosecco we were drinking and discovered that prosecco is actually from the Veneto originally, and if the bottle doesn't say Veneto on it then apparently it's not real prosecco. In order to support local winemakers we

then tried a chianti, and as we now had the courtyard to ourselves we wet the rim of our glasses, ran our fingers slowly round them and made them sing; two different crystal clear tones, bouncing off the walls and back to us. When we'd finished our drinks we asked whether we could go down to the cellars and see the collection of wines, advertised as consisting of 1600 different kinds. We were shown to the top of the steps and encouraged to enjoy ourselves. The steps down are wide and shallow and the walls and arched ceiling are bricked in awe-inspiringly beautiful curves within curves, perfectly rendered. Modern chrome and glass shelving units, uplit from the floor and by concealed lighting behind them held the displays of all the wines. We hardly looked at the wine, the rooms were so impressive. In one arm of this magnificent underground labyrinth we came across orderly rows of chairs in front of a head table, shelves of bottles lining the room from one end to the other. It must be the most elegant meeting room in the city, and is perhaps where wine experts give lectures. We wandered through the passages discovering rooms behind curtains, and little nooks, and as advertised, hundreds upon hundreds of bottles of wine. We decided that this, then, would be the venue for our last night treat dinner.

When we got back to the lobby there was no one at the desk so we wandered through to the dining room. Then we heard voices so we called out, but got no response. Then Sprat let out a mighty whistle and people fairly shot out of the kitchen, including the chef who had his wife and little girl with him, and he immediately went to great length – and a lot of gesturing – to explain to her that Sprat was the one who had whistled. He was obviously very impressed.

We made our reservation, thanked them profusely for a lovely evening, and set off home. Almost opposite the flat is a little church which is open sometimes, but not often. This evening a young gipsy girl, who we'd seen before in the town, was sitting outside the church, a permanent and angelic smile on her round face as she played the accordion and her boisterous lab-cross puppy chewed at the hem of her long skirts. We saw her several times after that, and always the same smile on her calm face, and always the boisterous puppy for company.

Tonight we decided to go back to the Fonti Guista because we both felt quite in need of some meat and we knew we would find something wonderful at our little trattoria. We ordered a plate of sausages and something called 'Overcooked pork with polenta' and it was sublime. We just ate our way through the plates of perfectly cooked meat, hardly a word passing between us. Coffee and the chef's own limoncello followed by another limoncello saw us right, and we just sat outside the cafe watching the evening begin to come to life; parties coming for dinner, young lovers hardly noticing what they ate and drank, an old couple eating slowly in a comfortable silence. Our perfect evening came to a close with a leisurely team effort of washing up when we got home, a cup of tea and a long hot shower.

In Italy, they add work and life on to food and wine.

Robin Leach

5.

Wednesday is market day in Siena and I had been looking forward to it immensely. We were up early and threw open the shutters to see the market all set up along La Lizza under the trees, and I knew it would stretch much further than that if it was anything like it used to be. Between us and the market was a bar where we were sure we would get coffee and brioche. When we saw the queue we almost changed our minds, but the line moved quickly and we soon saw why. Three beautiful young Italian girls were making coffee, fetching pastries, working the till, flirting with the customers and taking the next order without missing a beat. I listened to them calling cappuccino *cappucci,* so when it was our turn I tried it and in the blink of an eye we had our hot frothy cappucci and a fresh, flaky brioche. I've never heard it called that before and don't know whether it's peculiar to that team of Brilliant Baristas of Antico Bar La Lizza, or whether it's a Sienese thing.

The first stall we came to at the start of the market sold very high-end clothes: cashmere knitwear, soft leather bolero jackets, silk tunics. We fell on the clothes, but decided that we should look a bit more before making a choice. Quite quickly I remembered why Mum had come into the market every week and why she did all her shopping here. Table cloths, curtains, bolts of fabric, bath towels, kitchen utensils, wellie boots, pots and pans, clothes for every season, shoes, plants and food; everything for everyday life, in fact, and more besides. Even though we were quite early, we still had to elbow our way up to the tables and it took a force of will not to buy something from every table. Mostly like products could all be found together but just occasionally, between clothes stalls would be a food vendor and the one we got into conversation with was wonderful. A young woman with her daughter were selling baked goods of all sorts from a small, quite easy-to-miss stall. It turned out that she had been at university in Wales and now she and her husband and their collection of children and parents all live in the country and grow their own wheat which they mill and grind and bake and then sell at market. They make preserves too, but she told us that they actually make a living – quite a scant one, but a living all the same – from their baking. I promised to give her a mention – Podere La Lapole – and wished her very well.

At the end of the Lizza we could see that the stalls continued round under the wall and along the road where the fair lorries had driven past us, but as it was mostly plant, kitchen and hardware stalls, we decided to turn back the way we had come and make some purchases. One thing I really wanted to try and find was a t-shirt for my grandson, but not just any t-shirt. When we had all come to Italy for a family reunion many years ago, my brother had found the most wonderful t-shirt for his son on which was written the most extraordinary mix of English words that meant absolutely nothing, but  which may have meant something if translated back into Italian. Finally, to my joy, I found exactly what I was looking for and in the right size too. The words on it are:

Baby Did you MACHO YEARN Kismet! 56 ARE.DEPT. *Baker skeld* Trading luck. Written in different fonts and different colors it was quite the most extraordinary piece of clothing and I was thrilled with it.

Back at the first stall we had stopped at, Sprat decided on a heavenly cashmere tunic. I really wanted one of the silk tunics, but quite quickly it was obvious that nothing was going to fit; the very lovely stall holder waved her hand across her bosom while looking squarely at mine, and grinning, made some comment about *piu grande.* Still, for all that I hadn't come away empty handed and we started for home. Just as we were unlocking the door, it opened and out popped David. He was as startled as we were and he hastened to tell us as best he could that he had been to pick up the mail. When Sprat told him that she had lost her shirt but that it had been returned he looked quite puzzled, and thinking he hadn't understood the story, we told him again.

'It must be, er, how you say….. fantasme…' and he waved his hands about in the air, 'er… fantom….'

Sprat got it first.

'A ghost! Why?'

'The lady downstairs, she is very old, she stay all day in bed. She can no bring to you! Must be fantasme!'

We all laughed and made our farewells and Bruce lurched and rattled all the way to the top floor.

As we hadn't replenished our food stocks we went out for lunch, and had *tono e capri* – tuna and capers – panini, and a glass of cold white wine. The recipe for this delicacy is at the back. We walked slowly home and rewarded our morning's success with a little siesta.

* * * * *

The first thing to be done when we were up and out again was to go and buy our bus tickets for Florence for €15 each. We had decided to go to Pisa on Friday and spend the night, and fly home on Saturday. We went down and bought our tickets which would take us first to Florence in the afternoon and then on to Pisa, and with some shopping time before prosecco time, we went and bought some more little treasures from the shops whose opening times were so erratic we hadn't even been sure we'd find any of them open. A wonderful shop called Trame on Via Montanini not far from our flat, that sold silk ties, leather handbags and beautiful printed scarves got all our custom, and after a refreshing little chilled glass we went to our favorite Morbidi foods and bought the ultimate takeaway of veal stew, herby pork slices, gorgonzola, pecoriono, carcioffe, and cooked raddicio. Culinary heaven.

On the way home we decided to take a closer look at the splendid Piazza Salimbeni which is at the top of the Banci di Sopra and which we passed every day without really paying it any attention. A beautiful open doorway caught our eye so we decided to explore and see what it was. A government office, it appeared, with a notice saying no entry to unauthorised personnel.

Obviously we weren't the first people to decide to have a look. The enormous and very grand *palazzi* flanking the square are the head offices of the Monte di Paschi di Siena, where Dad used to bank. It's one of the oldest banks in the world, and contributes so much to the community in funds as well as employment that it's known as 'the city father.' The *palazzi* are marvels of architecture and the triple mullioned windows in the middle are typical of Sienese architecture. In the middle of the piazza is the statue of the archdeacon Sallustio Bandini, a champion of economic freedom, who died in 1780. It's a wonderful piazza and sitting on the steps of the statue and watching the world go by on Banchi di Sopra is an acceptable and pleasant way to spend a little time.

For supper we joined forces to make *panzanella* - just the way Mama used to make it – recipe in the back – and together with our picnic from Morbidi foods, we dined like queens.

From the kitchen at the back of the house we could hear noise in the street so we went through to the sitting room to see what was happening. Like many other Sienese we opened the shutters and windows and leant out to watch a pre-Palio parade of people going past, drums banging, whistles blowing, men, women and children singing and dancing and generally a good time being had by all. I remembered now that in the lead up to the Palio, each *contrada* is allowed their turn to parade through the streets, *contrada* flags flying, blood running high. Great fun, and especially fun watching it from a distance.

We both fell into bed exhausted but completely happy with our day's adventures.

Take only memories. Leave nothing but footprints.

Chief Seattle

6.

Holidays should be about little indulgences and the occasional act of decadence, like the chocolate croissant I had for breakfast, and like lying in bed and texting Sprat next door to see if she is awake yet. It was a later than usual start, and that's a holiday indulgence, too. Just off the Banchi di Sopra we had seen another food shop – Mood – which looked very swept up and inviting, so we gave it a go. Full of rather exotic foods and very expensive chocolate, we both bought a small bottle of balsamic glaze, among other things. Now that I know a bit more about balsamic vinegar and how it's made, I understand better why the price on our bottles made our eyes water. I haven't regretted buying it for a moment, and will be sad when it's finished. Oh dear, another trip to Italy for replenishment I suppose.

With the tone set for extravagant shopping, we moved further down towards the Campo to a

shop that has been there forever as far as I can tell
– Fonte dei Dolci – and which is, in my opinion,

the best sweet
shop to be
found. I noticed
how run down
its building
looked; grey with
dirt and neglect,
chipped plaster,
plants growing in
the gutters, wires
exposed and
pinned along the
top of the door,
and then a bright
and modern interior. I suppose, on reflection, that
a lot of the buildings are like that and, considering
their age and perpetual use, it is hardly surprising,
so I wonder why I noticed it just this once. Fonte
dei Dolci specialize in Sapori, the makers of
panforte which is the quintessential Tuscan nut
cake, often taken with a little coffee mid morning
and after a meal with a shot of limoncello. The
recipe in the back is the result of many
experiments to get it right, and I think we have
succeeded. Delicious. Sprat and I just moved
slowly up and down the shelves filling our arms
with delights. Baci chocolates, panforte, licorice
and fruit lozenges in the most beautiful boxes,

wafer thin rounds of nougat in sturdy plastic boxes with beautiful labels, packets of amoretti, chocolate covered coffee beans, in fact anything that took our fancy. We felt a bit embarrassed by our excessive shopping but I'm sure we aren't the first nor will we be the last to go crazy on such delights.

With a few ceramic items still on our list, we went and got those, and then knowing how much we'd pay we still decided to go into the Campo for one last cappuccino. The sun was hot, the cafes were bustling, and apart from one group of tourists resting in the shade of the Torre di Mangia at the bottom of the square, there  were really very few people in the Campo, certainly compared with St Mark's in Venice. What a joy to be able to go to the Fonte Gaia and stand, almost alone, at the railings and look at the amazing detail of the carved figures all around the pool and the rather patient looking marble dogs lying on their shelves over the water. A little trickle of water comes out of each of their mouths while about a dozen heat-dazed pigeons perch on the feet of the statues and on the dogs' heads. The pool must have the coins cleaned out of it on a regular basis or, judging by the number in there, it would be more coin than water by now. While we sat idly in the sun watching the world around us, a wedding party came out of the *palazzo publico*.

All looking handsome and beautiful, they posed for their photos, oblivious or at least unperturbed by all the onlookers.

Laden with all our wonderful shopping we wandered slowly home and had a lunch of all the delicacies left in the fridge; cheese and olives and tomatoes and cold meat with the fresh foccacia we had just bought, and after admiring all our gifts which we had laid out in the sitting room, we were exhausted enough for another siesta.

* * * * *

'I think we should go to the Duomo this afternoon.'

'Actually' Sprat pointed out 'we *must* go this afternoon or we won't go at all and we'll be really sorry we didn't.' And really it was a case of saving the best till last.

Built in stripes of black and white marble, it is quite the most astonishing building to look at.

Started in the 13th century, it has been added to and changed over the centuries and is quite unlike any other church I have seen in Italy. But wonderful though the facade is, it's the floor of the cathedral that wins the day. Consisting of 56 mosaic panels done in black and white and dark red marble

intarsia, it is quite the most extraordinary work. It took hundreds of years to complete and covers the entire floor of the cathedral, but many of the very early panels are covered and protected for most of the year, only being on display for about two months a year, during the Palio and into September. But no mind, there are enough to look at and to be overwhelmed by. As if that wasn't enough to take in, the black and white striped columns soar upwards to support domes of rich blue painted with hundreds of gold stars. There are fabulous works of art in the cathedral too – imagine walking round the corner and coming face to face with Caravaggio's Shepherd Boy, on loan from Rome and completely unadvertised, allowing us a full, leisurely view as though it had been cordoned off just for us. But the floor, ceilings and the astounding carved octagonal pulpit were about all we could absorb, and the bits we missed will have to wait till next time; our heads were full and spinning and we needed a rest from it all. As we left the Duomo by the main door, I pointed across the square to a huge, nondescript building opposite us and said

'That was the hospital. It's where Dad was when he was so sick. Apparently the walls are all covered with frescoes which have been completely left alone.'

'Hmm - 'elf and safety wouldn't allow that in England, would they? How lovely to lie in bed and have something like that to look at.' Now an arts centre and exhibition space, the Santa Maria della Scala was founded in the 9th century and in its day was one of the most important hospitals in the world. The frescos, depicting scenes of the history of the hospital, are by Domenico di Bartolo.

We retraced our steps down the hill towards the Campo and from our favoured ice cream shop we bought two little tubs and went and sat on the steps of what is actually a bank. The steps are the width of the building, and between the columns at the top of the steps are the most ornate wrought iron railings and gate. These protect a portico with a mosaic floor and a ceiling of quite the most astonishing work; carved and gilded and painted in equal measure, it's no wonder that passersby kept stopping right beside us to photograph it.

As this would quite likely be our last time down at this end of town, we decided we would try to find a new way home, one more little explore. We set off up the Banchi di Sopra and then at the first opportunity we turned right, and very quickly found ourselves in unfamiliar territory. We wandered along, hardly meeting anyone, and were just admiring a little plaque high up on the wall which told us which *contrada* we were in, when a little old lady who was passing stopped and asked us what we were looking for. We tried to tell her we weren't looking for anything in particular, but were just admiring the plaque which we pointed to. She misunderstood this, and thinking we were looking at the street sign, immediately started directing us somewhere. We understood ' go down here' as she pointed down the street we were facing, and then something about Santa Francesco, and because we couldn't make her understand that we weren't really looking for anything we nodded and smiled and thanked her and set off in the direction she sent us. At the end of the street was a rather steep street crossing it, and directly ahead of us a restaurant with tables and umbrellas outside it. We stood and looked at it for a moment, wondering what it was about it that was so strange and then we realised; the legs of the chairs and tables had been cut, one set shorter than the

other, so they sat perfectly straight on the steep slope of the road. A man was sitting reading a paper at one of the tables, the back legs of his chair two inches shorter than the front legs. Ingenious. We set off down the hill and turned immediately to our left, knowing we were heading in the general direction of the flat. Without any warning, the narrow streets grew wider, the buildings fell away revealing a wide open, empty forecourt and there, in all its glory, was the Basilica di San Francesco. Much bigger than San Domenico, it is attached to numerous other imposing buildings all of which are now part of the university. We crossed the forecourt, feeling very small and insignificant, and at the door stopped to look at the confetti littering the ground in front of the door. Then something caught my eye and I bent to pick it up; a tiny – perhaps 2" long – €500 note! It was all part of the confetti and I suppose this was the modern version of showering the happy couple with money. I couldn't resist, and I smile every time I use my little confetti bookmark.

Like San Domenico, the interior of San Francesco was cavernous and dark and almost completely devoid of seating. At the far end of the huge hall we could see benches had been put in front of the altar, and a wedding was in progress. We couldn't hear a word that was being said, it was all so far away, but the bride's bright white dress glowed in the  dim light. We felt as though we were intruding so we quietly left without looking at any of the frescoes. Back in the sunshine we headed in what we knew to be the general direction of the flat. Little shops and restaurants, courtyards and fountains and churches are to be seen round every corner, on every street, and then suddenly,

'Look at that!'

On the side of a building – obviously a house – was a window in which a young girl was standing, naked from the waist up. She was half hidden by the curtain she was holding open, and she gazed out onto the street, unmoving.

'Is she real? I mean really carved, or is she painted?'

We couldn't get quite close enough to see whether she was carved or a brilliant piece of trompe l'oeile, made to look like marble and stone and brick, but after studying her from any angle we could find, we both came away fairly convinced she was the most wonderful piece of carving. I wonder if I'd ever be able to find her again.

* * * * *

If I had lain down when we got home I probably would have slept through till the next day, but we had an important date to keep, so I started packing instead. Our table at the Enoteca was booked for 7.30 and we were only a little late; by Italian standards safe to say we were really on time.

The courtyard was full of gentle evening light, the air warm enough to need no shawls and there was only one other couple there with us. We ordered our prosecco and then spent ages trying to decide what to eat. The menu was fantastic, and it was important that we weren't in any hurry because it would have spoiled the whole amazing event.

Our waiter for the evening was the sommelier himself, and what a lovely gent he was. Wavy iron grey hair, weathered skin and the brightest twinkle in his eye. When our delectable starters arrived – sliced figs with walnut panforte, pear and a variety of cheeses – Sprat looked at hers and said to me – as an inside joke –

'Oh well, that's rubbish.' Without missing a beat he stood back slightly and said

'Yes, you weel not enjoy eet at all!'

We both looked up at him, a trifle startled, and got our first sighting of the wicked twinkle. It was going to be an entertaining evening.

We slowly ate our way through quite the most sublime meal of thyme perfumed chicken with red tropea onions, the prosecco having given way to a bottle of the sommelier's own choice of Chianti. For dessert we both had *cantucci*, *pan del pescatore* and *vin santo* which was served in perfect miniaturised martini glasses so not a drop was wasted because it couldn't be reached, and when we were unwilling – nay, unable – to talk, out came our waiter with two little glasses of freezing cold limoncello and two more *cantucci*.

'The chef's own limoncello – he would like you to try it.' So we did, and then unsure of whether we'd really liked it, we agreed to just one more taste trial.

We've established that our last night's meal is to be enjoyed without thought for the bill, and this is exactly what we did tonight. Imagine our surprise and disbelief when the bill arrived and it was a measly €88. Amazing, and unsung. We gathered ourselves together to leave at 10 o'clock, and only then were the next diners arriving. We had had the whole terrace and all the staff to ourselves, and now the poor things really had to start work as a party of 30 started arriving. It would be a late night for some!

On our way out we went to the manager's desk to see if we could find him and thank him for the most wonderful evening. With all his staff in bow ties and black suits, he was dressed, somewhat incongruously, in jeans and a jean jacket. We told him how much we had enjoyed our evening, that we travel and write, and we would give the Enoteca a huge fanfare in the book. More important to him, though, was a big write-up in TripAdvisor. Oh well, fledgling ducks only so why should he be impressed? We did ask for the menu, and only on the strength of our promising to write the review did he give us a copy.

'Do not tell my chef!' he urged us, 'he can be very..... *jealous!*'

Walking home through the park and past the bars holds no sort of threat whatever. We were probably more aware of our surroundings too because this was our last night and it's a sad time when you acknowledge that this might actually be the last time. We were quite subdued tidying up the kitchen and talking quietly about our travel plans for the next day, but that didn't prevent either of us enjoying one last wonderfully comfortable night in our beloved Siena.

You may have the universe if I may have Italy.

Giuseppe Verdi

7.

We left the keys on the beautiful carved sideboard, took our last ride in Bruce and after the usual perfect breakfast, crossed the road and caught our bus to Florence.

The drive to Florence took just under an hour and a half, and was in a much more comfortable bus than the one we had come from Pisa to Siena in. We raced down the motorway, only glimpsing the wonderful countryside as we went. The poppies still lit up the side of the road, the needle pines and small towns – or big houses – on the tops of the hills reminded us we were still in Tuscany, but it's not the best way to see the country. When the bus pulled into the bus depot in Florence, the first order of the day was to find a loo and then get some lunch. The sandwiches we bought at the tired little cafe counter didn't do anything for the reputation of Italian cuisine but they would sustain us as far as Pisa. And then we had our own version of Groundhog Day with the bus service. We realised quite quickly we were standing in the wrong queue for the Pisa bus so we went and asked the ticket seller. Just as in Pisa, she barely looked at us, waved vaguely over her right shoulder, muttered something about 'outside' and went to the next customer. Off we went, out onto the street. We looked at some lovely little shops as we wandered along but it's hard to get into shopping mode when all you're worried about is finding where your bus might be, let alone actually catching it. A series of enquiries of random people took us up into a shopping mall, round and out the other side which landed us up straight across the road from the bus depot we had just left. Easy when you know how...

We were the only people there, there wasn't even a bus, but eventually one arrived and when the driver got out we saw to our surprise that it was one of the drivers that Sprat had talked to at Pisa airport when we arrived; he was the one who had waved her away to the other end of the bus depot and had thus started the Round Of the Buses. The good thing was that we could be pretty certain this would be our bus back to Pisa. We were allowed to load our suitcases – unaided of course – into the hold and to get onto the bus and find a seat. Lessons learned, we took the two front seats so we'd have the best view on the journey. We wanted to eat our uninviting but necessary panini but were discouraged from doing so on the bus and had to get off to eat. Sprat offered to go back into the mall and get us each a coffee and while she was gone, people and buses began appearing all around us, the shouting and waving and asking and telling started in earnest and I was beginning to worry that I'd lost Sprat. By the time she reappeared our bus was filling up and our driver was getting anxious to start out, but a passenger had mislaid his ticket and was scrabbling feebly through all the rubbish in his man bag; another decided he absolutely had to go to the loo and took off, leaving all his kit on his seat, and another who had a long and protracted farewell to deal with, all delayed the whole show from getting on the road, and our driver got more and more fed up, only just managing to remain civil. Sprat and I had eaten, been to the loo, had a coffee, had front seats and no deadline, so we let the dramas all unfold around us and let ourselves be entertained. Eventually everyone was accounted for, the bus inspector had counted us all more than once and tallied our numbers to the tickets he had in his hand, and we were ready to go.

Just as we were pulling out into the traffic, I glanced over to my left and there, peeping out from behind building site barricades and modern blocks of flats I spied the dome of the very famous cathedral of Florence, Santa Maria del Fiore. I quickly took what is probably the worst picture ever taken of this magnificent building. Anxious to make up for lost time, our driver fairly threw the bus round the corners and into the fray, barely missing some crossing pedestrians and eliciting the wrath of another motorist. All the naughty Italian words I'd learned at school are absolutely correct – we heard every single one of them in quick succession as our driver put the rest of the traffic in its place. Once out of the city he calmed down, and the drive to Pisa was otherwise uneventful. Like the journey to Florence, there isn't much to see except new-build houses, warehouses and factories and a lot of cars being driven very fast. We were quite relieved to arrive in Pisa just over an hour later, and the driver of the taxi we caught to take us to our hotel did so in a calm and orderly fashion. We had a chance to really look around us and see that Pisa, in spite of its reputation as a heaving hoards tourist destination, is a lovely little town and very ancient.

I had booked a hotel a short drive from the airport and a reasonable walk from the leaning tower, reckoning half way between the two to be the most likely to work. The lobby of the hotel looked lovely, but the staff were all a bit distracted and inefficient and it turned out to be because it had only just re-opened and was all still being put back together after a refurb.

Our room was absolutely basic – two

boarding school beds – nondescript bedside tables and a small bathroom, but it was all we needed for one night. We put down our bags and went out again, heading for the leaning tower which I had last seen in 1987 before tourists had really cottoned to Italy in any big way. Walking through the town was lovely; late afternoon, warm but not hot, and the time of year when gardens have begun to bloom, trees are all covered in leaves, and fresh bright window pots have been planted. As with every Italian town, there are secret alleys with wonderful palazzi at the end of them, and the occasional walled garden with a

monumental, ancient house set right back among the old growth trees – always surprising in the heart of a busy city. As we got closer to the tower, the temporary market stands increased in number, all selling miniatures of the tower and all the other tat that goes with it. I was surprised and amazed by the changes that had come about since I was last here all that time ago. The square in front of the tower beside the church is still there of course, but now it's ringed with vendors stalls. Big grass lawns have been planted, surrounded by chain on steel poles with wide concrete paths between them. Signs urge you to keep off the grass, of course. The tower itself, magnificent anyway and even more so at its jaunty angle, is pristine. Bright creamy and pale grey marble glowing in the evening light, and to my surprise only two people right up at the top of the tower. I had expected to see a line of brave souls snaking round the tower, which still only has barriers on the top three levels, all the others open to the ground and rather scary to climb. Perhaps it was too late in the day for new climbers, and those who were up would soon have to come down. Countless sightseers all around the grounds, people taking photographs as usual of their friends pretending to push the tower over, others standing with their hand out and looking as though they are holding the tower up. Sprat and I got as close to the tower as we could and wondered at the beauty of it, but quite quickly decided we would rather find somewhere for supper and have a peaceful, warm evening. We found the restaurant that had been recommended by the receptionist at the hotel and chose a table outside, near the street so we could watch the world passing by. We lasted exactly as long as it takes to drink a glass of very mediocre wine. The music was unbearably loud, the staff couldn't care less about their discerning customers – numbed and inured to crass and indifferent tourists I'm sure – so we paid our bill and set off away from the tower and towards the town to look for somewhere more local to eat. We were in a strange part of town, mostly residential and not very Italian looking somehow, but eventually the road opened out and opposite the huge arch in the wall that leads the traffic out of the city, we found a little restaurant called Pietro Maffi; outside was a platform with half a dozen tables over which was a blue and white awning. We chose the one we wanted and from the very nice and interested waiter we ordered our drinks and supper and had a wonderful calm, properly Italian evening, far from the madding crowds. By the time we left, every table was occupied and the restaurant was full too. Popular choice, obviously.

* * * * *

There's something quite lovely about lying in bed talking quietly and then getting so close to being asleep that you don't know whether you have really replied or just thought you did. We drifted off thus on our last night, having made the decision to gamble between being eaten alive by mosquitoes and having some fresh air in the room. We opened the dense wire screen about half way and took our chances. In the morning we found we had both been well bitten, but we'd had a cool and fairly comfortable night and been unaware of the blood letting, so it was worth it.

Breakfast was surprisingly nice in the little back garden in the cool morning, and then it was time to get to the airport, and the rhythm of the holiday changes; there are places to be at required times, queues to stand in, and in an airport like Pisa, enormous amounts of patience to be found and used. It's difficult not to let the last hours of a holiday be the presiding memory of the trip, and on the plane home we always talk about the most impressive, the funniest, and the most interesting bits so we land on home soil with all that fresh in our minds and preserved as it should be. I had made a conscious decision not to go back to the Cava where Mum and Dad had made such an amazing life for themselves – and for us when we could partake – and I'm not sorry because the memory of the little house, the hard work, chickens, cats, geese, vegetable garden, vineyards, great company and fabulous food are preserved as they are.

As we flew out of Pisa and said our goodbyes to Siena, I was reminded of the best description of Siena that I had read; *it is a city with the psychology of a village and the grandeur of a nation.*

The love affair is over, but I will be in love forever.

Ciao, Siena, e grazi per tutti.

Ricette.

Sprat: I became interested in cooking from my grandmother who, when she married, didn't know how to boil an egg. So she chose a cookery book and started at page one and worked her way through. She became a fabulous self-taught cook and my sister and I stayed with her regularly as our mother worked full time, so we had the benefit of her experience. She used to be able to make cream out of butter. I still think it's magic.

I trained and worked as a chef until I married and eventually completed an illustration degree. Unsurprisingly, most of my illustrations are of food.

Phil: My culinary journey has been less formal. My Mum was the most wonderful cook – she could have taught Nigel Slater everything about cooking with what you've got on hand – and that's become my style of cooking. But following a recipe is a relief – someone else has made all the decisions about how it should be done! I think this might be part of the reason why I have such a love for Italian food; pasta and gnocchi sauces, frittata, risotto, pizza, panini – they can all be made simply delicious with whatever you have to hand. Just my kind of cooking.

We talk about recipes, swap recipes and love Italian food particularly. I don't understand why we're not the size of a house.

These recipes are well tested by both of us, separately and together, and while most are based on or inspired by what we ate in Siena, a few are just because they're Italian and completely delicious.

Parmesan Biscuits

We didn't discover these in Siena but they are
made with Parmesan cheese, so therefore they
qualify in our view. The recipe belongs to Simon
Hopkinson who I think is the best chef on TV
(and off). These biscuits are melting, savoury little
discs of joy.

A food processor is the easiest thing to use or a
mixer with the cake-making paddle. I've used
both and they work well but you can do it by
hand too.

Ingredients

100g unsalted butter, cut into small chunks

100g of plain flour

A pinch of salt

A good pinch of cayenne pepper

1 heaped tsp of English mustard powder

50g finely grated parmesan, plus a little extra

1 small beaten egg for glazing

Method

Oven 180°C/350°F/G4

Lightly grease an oven tray.

Put the butter, flour, cheese, salt, peppers and mustard powder into the mixer bowl. Use the pulse button with the processor or at medium speed with a mixer until the mix just comes together.

Wrap in cling film and cool in the fridge for at least 30 minutes.

Roll out the pastry on a lightly floured board to roughly the thickness of a two pound coin (or a euro)

Stamp out small biscuits with a pastry cutter and arrange on the greased baking tray.

Brush each biscuit with beaten egg and sprinkle with a little of the extra parmesan

Bake for ten minutes until golden.

Cool on a wire tray.

Eat them all.

Tuna and Caper Panini
(or Ciabatta)

This is such simple lunchtime food and it is one of those dishes that you don't believe will be much of anything but which turns out to be really delicious. It sounds as though it's going to be rather dry, but it won't be – don't be tempted to add mayonnaise to this because it spoils its lovely flavour and texture.

Serves 1

Ingredients

1 small tin of tuna

1 level tbsp of capers - either in brine and drained, or the sort that comes in a jar with salt crystals (my favourite)

1 panino or half a ciabatta loaf

Olive oil

Method

Split the roll or bread horizontally and toast lightly. Drizzle with a little olive oil.

Mix the drained tuna and the capers together, and fill the panino or ciabatta roll.

Eat it!

Rich Tomato Sauce

Everyone has their favourite tomato sauce recipe
and this is mine. It comes from the recipe book
that I inherited from a cookery school in Tuscany.
Don't be tempted to leave the butter out because
it makes it very mellow. These quantities make
about a litre and I freeze it in small batches and
have it with pasta when I want a quick delicious
lunch.

Ingredients

1 celery stalk, finely chopped

1 carrot chopped into tiny pieces

1 clove of garlic, finely chopped

A large handful of flat leaf parsley, finely chopped

1 small onion, peeled and finely chopped

A small bunch of basil torn into pieces

750g of well flavoured fresh tomatoes, deseeded and chopped *or* 750g of tinned Italian tomatoes drained and chopped

2 tbsp sundried tomato paste

2 tbsp olive oil

2 tbsp unsalted butter

Method

Heat the oven to 180°C/350°F/G4

Put the tomatoes into a large casserole with the tomato paste and stir until blended together.

Sprinkle with carrots on top, then in layers, the celery, onion, garlic and then the herbs. Don't mix it yet.

Pour the olive oil on the top and bring it to just below boiling on the stove top. Transfer the casserole to the oven heated to 180°C for about an hour or until all the vegetables are soft.

At this stage, you can either pulse it in a food processor to get it smoother or leave it as it is.

Add the butter and stir it through and then simmer on the stove until it is thickish which will take about ten minutes. Take care that it doesn't stick in the pan. Check the seasoning.

Orange Vinaigrette for a Green Salad.

This is a sweeter dressing than the normal vinaigrette and ideal as a fresh tasting foil for punchy main courses. It's lovely on a green salad with peppery leaves such as watercress.

Ingredients

Segments of one orange

Juice of an additional half an orange

2 heaped tsp Dijon mustard

1 tsp honey

Salt and pepper

Half and half olive and sunflower oil - about 150ml in total

Method

Segment one of the oranges into your green salad. (Removing the skin)

To make the dressing, mix together in a bowl the juice of the remaining half orange, the mustard, honey, salt and pepper. Gradually whisk in the oil in a steady thin stream until you get a thick vinaigrette. Add more oil if you like it thicker. Taste it to check the seasoning.

Panzanella

Panzanella is a family recipe in that everyone has their own version, but this is the recipe that Phil's Mum, Honi, was taught in Tuscany by a native Tuscan so it's the perfect one, in my view. It is a way to use up stale bread and a glut of tomatoes, basically, but all sorts of things can be added. We have copied Honi's version and hope you'll agree that it is just perfect.

This is enough for two as a main dish or for four as a side salad.

Ingredients

Four fresh, medium tomatoes, skinned and and de-seeded and cut up small.

One good sized mild onion, peeled and chopped into small cubes

Half a large or a whole small cucumber, chopped in small cubes

4oz of coarse breadcrumbs from a stale rustic loaf – we used ciabatta.

Ground black pepper, salt

Olive oil

Vinegar – we used a mild rice vinegar.

A good-sized bunch of chopped fresh flat leaf parsley.

Method

Gently toss all the diced vegetables and parsley together in a bowl with the salt and pepper.

Add the breadcrumbs and drizzle over about 2 tbsp of oil and about a tbsp of the vinegar.

Gently toss it all together; it should be moist but not soggy.

It's lovely to eat straight away, but it can be left for about 15 mins for the bread to soak up the juices. Any longer, and it might go soggy, which would spoil it.

One-Pot Pasta

You are going to have to trust us with this one. It sounds so unlikely, but always results in a fabulously flavoured pasta dish with just the right amount of sauce. We used tinned tomatoes here because fresh, supermarket tomatoes often don't have enough flavour. If you are cooking this in Italy, use their glorious fresh ones. (I was in a supermarket in England recently and noticed that the label on their specialist tomatoes read 'grown for flavour'. I'm still pondering that one.)

Serves 4

Ingredients

200g linguine (dried, not fresh)

One 400g tin chopped tomatoes with herbs or garlic or whatever you like.

4 cloves of garlic sliced thinly

Bunch of fresh basil if you have it, otherwise a good tsp of dried basil

2 tsp of oregano – we put thyme in ours but really any of those lovely herbs will do, they make their own variation on the theme.

One large onion, thinly sliced

4 cups vegetable broth – one cube or one stock pot

Drizzle of oil

Salt and pepper

A shake of red chilli flakes

1 generous tablespoon of sun dried tomato paste

Method

You'll need quite a good sized hob-top pot with a lid.

Peel and cut your onion and put in the pot.

Peel and slice the garlic and add to the onion.

Pour in the tin of tomatoes or chopped fresh tomatoes, then add the broth, tomato paste, basil, salt and pepper, chilli flakes and the pasta. I don't break the pasta because I like it long for winding round my fork, but if you break it in half then you don't have to stand over the pot waiting for the pasta to soften enough to be pushed into the liquid.

Bring it to a steady boil, and stir it occasionally to stop anything sticking and to keep the flavours mixed.

By the time the liquid has almost boiled away the linguine will be cooked. You want it to look just like pasta covered with a nice moist sauce.

Serve with grated Parmesan and be amazed!

Chicken with Mascarpone

My husband has always professed to hate both pasta and cooked tomatoes. When he turned forty, we went to Tuscany for a holiday at a villa where you could either learn to cook Italian food or work with a professional artist for a week. I rather meanly forced him to do the cookery course, hoping that he would learn to love pasta and cooked tomatoes like any sane person. It didn't work, but he learnt this recipe which is just gorgeous and very easy. (I did the art course and ended up doing an art degree – but that's another story).

Serves 2

Ingredients

A good quality chicken breast for each person (the quality really matters here)

1 scant tbsp of very finely chopped rosemary leaves

3 tbsp of mascarpone

3 tbsp of crème fraîche

I scant tbsp of freshly squeezed lemon juice and the zest of half a lemon

Salt

Pepper

Method

In a frying pan melt a knob of butter with a tbsp of olive oil. Brown the chicken breasts on both sides. Put them into an oven-proof dish.

In a bowl, mix together the rosemary, mascarpone, crème fraîche, lemon juice and zest, salt and pepper, and the juices from the pan that you fried the chicken in.

Spread this sauce over the chicken breasts, cover with foil and put it in the oven at about 220˚C/425˚F/G7 for 20 to 25 minutes.

Take it out of the oven and slice through one chicken breast to make sure it's cooked. If it's pink, put it back for 5 more minutes.

When it's cooked, put the chicken breasts on a plate, cover with foil and leave them to rest.

Scrape all the sauce that the chicken cooked in into a little sauce pan. Taste for seasoning. If you want more sauce add a little more crème fraîche.

Keep the sauce warm on a very low heat. Then cut the chicken breasts into slices and arrange on the plates. Any chicken juices that have gathered on the plate can be stirred into the sauce.

Pour the sauce over the chicken, dividing evenly, and serve.

We served this with a very simple tomato and onion salad; four nice sized ripe tomatoes, one red onion and some cubed feta. Drizzle with olive oil, add fresh or dried basil and a grind of black pepper, toss and serve.

This makes a very light meal. If you want to make it a bit more substantial serve with boiled baby potatoes or a lovely rustic type bread.

Lemon and Parsley Tortellini

Fresh tortellini are easy to find in supermarkets. It's a great standby and can be frozen. This simple recipe takes shop-bought fresh pasta to another level.

Serves 2 generously

Ingredients

Juice and zest of one lemon

5 tbsp olive oil

Large bunch of fresh flat leaf parsley, chopped

100g grated Parmesan

1 packet of fresh tortellini

Salt and pepper

Method

Squeeze the lemon into a large bowl and add the finely grated zest. Add the olive oil, parsley, salt and pepper to taste. Add the Parmesan, saving a little for garnishing. Mix all together.

Boil the tortellini according to the directions on the packet. Drain when ready and toss into the bowl with the dressing, not the other way round. Mix gently so the tortellini is coated in the sauce, but be careful not to break the little parcels.

This is a lovely meal on its own, but we had a green salad with an orange dressing (recipe follows).

Buon appetito!

Panforte

This is the delicious and quintessentially Sienese sweet that can be eaten anytime - or all the time - with coffee, for dessert or as a vaguely healthy snack. It's very easy to make once you have the right recipe. We've tested many recipes and this is the best one we've found.

Ingredients

Butter, to grease

100g each ready-to-eat dried apricots, mixed peel and walnuts

175g runny honey

200g light brown soft sugar

Large pinch each ground cloves and nutmeg

1 1/2 tsp ground cinnamon

2 1/2 tbsp plain flour

100g each whole hazelnuts and almonds

175g ground almonds

Icing sugar to dust

Method

Preheat oven to 160°C/320°F/G3.

Grease a 20.5cm (8") round tin and line with baking parchment. Traditionally, rice paper is used and we recommend this because the bottom is quite sticky.

Chop apricots, mixed peel and walnuts if not already chopped.

In a large pan, melt the honey and brown sugar until dissolved and bring it only just to the boil. Be careful not to let it boil for more than a few seconds or you will have a gluey mess at the end that whips out fillings faster than a dentist.

Stir in ground cloves, grated nutmeg, 1tsp cinnamon and 2 tbsp of the flour and stir through thoroughly.

Take the pan off heat and stir in the hazelnuts, whole almonds and ground almonds and chopped fruit. The mixture will be very stiff. Press the mixture into the prepared tin.

In a small bowl mix the remaining 1/2 tsp of cinnamon and the remaining 1/2 tbsp of flour.

Dust this over the pan forte mixture and bake for 40 minutes until slightly risen.

Don't be tempted to take it out before the time is up - it's impossible to tell whether it's properly cooked just by looking.

Brush off any excess flour mixture and leave in the tin until completely cool. Then dust with icing sugar and cut small wedges to serve. It's very rich and a small slice will - often - be enough.

Dolce and a Party Trick

When it comes to puddings, we had the lovely, complicated stuff only when we went out to eat – because when you're on holiday, why put yourself through the hassle of making Tiramisu or Tart di limone when you could be wandering in the sun or having a siesta? It's fine to get deserts from patisseries anyway - that's what most people do.

The seasonal fresh fruit is lovely just on its own, or maybe have a spread of small, easy to buy (or make) sweet things.

At various times, we had panforte with our coffee, cantoccini dipped in vin santo, or affogatto – which is a scoop of the best vanilla ice cream with strong espresso poured over the top. All of these delights are easily produced at home and they make wonderful desserts.

The Party Trick
(best done outside in the garden on a warm evening)

One of the nicest things to have with your after dinner coffee are crisp, almondy amoretti biscuits. If you want to impress your friends, make sure you buy the ones that are individually wrapped in Italian tissue-type papers.

After eating these lovely things, save the papers and go into the garden with a plate and a box of matches. Make a tube shape out of an amoretti paper and stand it upright on the plate. Light a match and touch it to the top of the little tube and stand back and watch to the very end..........

Acknowledgements

The creation of this book amounts to the team effort, and Sprat and I would never have made it fly without the help of our brilliant, kind and patient editor, Anna Coryndon, our brilliant, supportive and patient illustrator, Matthew Dunn (www.mdartist.co.uk) and our long-suffering and clever book designer, Matt Maguire (www.candescentpress.co.uk). Add to the mix our dear husbands, R & R, and the team is complete. Thank you all.

33964048R00070

Printed in Great Britain
by Amazon